THE CRYSTAL BALL

by
Sibyl Ferguson

SAMUEL WEISER, INC.

York Beach, Maine

First published in 1979 by
Samuel Weiser, Inc.
Box 612
York Beach, Maine 03910

99
14 13 12 11 10

ISBN 0-87728-483-0
BJ

Printed in the United States of America

The paper used in this publication meets the minimum requirements of the American National Standard for Permanence of Paper for Printed Library Materials Z39.48-1984.

Contents

The Crystal Ball 5
Health and the Crystal Ball 6
Where and How to House the Crystal Ball 6
How to Use the Crystal Ball 8
Interpretation of Phenomena Seen in the Crystal Ball 9
The Search for the Secret of Crystal Gazing 11
Early Advocates of the Crystal Ball 14
Bibliography 14

The Crystal Ball

While the crystal ball is a little understood mode of divination, it is one method, if not the most enticing, of augury. Probably there are as many definitions of crystal balls as there are opinionated people. However, it is usual to group these individuals into three categories—the Ancients, the Geologists, and the Seers or Scryers.

The Ancients supposed crystals to be congealed water or ice petrified by some long-continued natural process. These long-ago people invoked the power of the crystal to change the fate of individuals, and often to modify the course of a country's events. It is reported that Pliny, the Elder (23-79) subscribed to this belief, and that Seneca (4 B.C.?-65 A.D.) supported his opinion. This belief extended well into the Middle Ages. Even today under the tundra of Northern America may be found a buried sheet of ice formed by clear spring water which rises from the rocks beneath the alluvial deposits at the Zone of Freezing. This crystosphene, as it is designated, might easily deceive individuals today, had not the Ancients' belief been refuted by the Geologists.

The Geologist, to put it briefly and simply, is a person who specializes in the history of the earth as recorded in the rocks. The Geologist defines a crystal as a body formed by the solidification of a chemical or compound. It is either colorless or only slightly tinged with color. It is known as quartz or rock-crystal. The Geologist is a very practical person who, generally, does not lean toward the Occult. To him a crystal is a crystal is a crystal. True, but is there anyone who is able to forget that magical device—the first radio? It was known as a *crystal* set for its receiver had a *crystal* detector. All instruments worthy of being classed as magical do affect the future of humanity. Need it be pointed out to anyone the undreamed future of that original *crystal* radio set?

The Seer or Scryer sees the Crystal Ball very differently. He looks upon it as the Generic Ovum in whose transparent, unfathomable depth lies the whole of creation. In it is preserved all terrestrial energy in its myriad forms. The Seer is a person credited with extraordinary moral and spiritual insight, and practices crystallomancy or divination through gazing into the Crystal Ball.

Health and the Crystal Ball

One of the first concerns confronting those desirous of becoming Seers is health. The vigor and robustness of an athlete are *not* a requisite. The essentials are a reasonably sound mind and body. To attain a reliable and high stage of perception, a healthy brain, a steady heart, and lungs capable of deep breathing are indispensable. The Scryer remains calm and unmoved by trivialities under any circumstance.

Extensive observation by reliable medical men has shown conclusively that Crystal Gazing has no ill effect on the Scryer's health.

One of the most renowned Scryers, Miss Goodrich-Freer, is quoted as saying, "The four years during which I have carried on experiments in crystal-gazing have been among the healthiest of my life."

The writings of some of the great occultists have presented a quite different opinion. To name a few, both F. Podmore and F.W.H. Myers felt Crystal Gazing had no adverse effect on the health of the Seer. Their continued investigations along with those of other reputable authors presented a most encouraging picture. Quite the reverse became noticeable as the Seer's development progressed. Gradually, uncertainty or apparent discomfort was replaced by a stable, serene attitude. The mental efficiency was unmistakably enhanced.

Where and How to House the Crystal Ball

A Crystal Ball is not a toy, and it should be treated with great respect and deference. If the owner is seriously considering Seership, it is important to house it in a room of its own.

A small room is preferable, and it should be kept impeccably clean. This applies to the entire room—floors, walls, and windows, as well as the furnishings. Anything that might distract the attention should be eliminated.

The furnishings should be kept simple and down to a minimum. A small, sturdy table to hold the Crystal Ball, and two unpretentious but comfortable chairs should be sufficient. However, if the Seer finds it necessary to record what the Crystal Ball has revealed, a small chest of drawers to accommodate stationery may be added.

KEEP THE CRYSTAL BALL CLEAN! This is not a rule. It is a *command.* When its surface becomes soiled, make a mild solution of luke-warm water and triple-milled soap in a small basin. Rest the Crystal Ball on a square of white flannel, which has been placed on the bottom of the basin. Gently wash the Crystal Ball to remove all trace of soil. Then rinse in a solution of alcohol and water, or preferably a solution of vinegar and water. Dry with a soft linen cloth, and polish with a piece of chamois kept for that purpose.

As has been said already, the Crystal Ball is not a toy to be handled indiscriminately by anyone out of curiosity. Ideally, only the Seer's hands should touch it. The dedicated Scryer magnetizes the Crystal Ball by passing the right hand over it to impart strength and might. Then the action should be repeated with the left hand to transmit more sensitiveness. Generally, when the Seer is alone this exercise is carried on for five minutes at several periods during the day. Then, too, magnetism from the transcendental ethers collect on the surface of the Crystal Ball as the Seer gazes fixedly upon it. To put it simply in the words of the modern idiom, this is comparable to "recharging the battery."

It can be readily understood that handling by the curious actually destroys the sensitiveness of the Crystal Ball. As has been pointed out, magnetism collects on the surface of this extremely responsive instrument. However, it is conceded the Crystal Ball is an inanimate object. It is powerless to say, "I shall allow only the Seer's magnetism to collect on my surface." It is unable to move away from an alien intruder. Its power is to reveal to a sensitive that which lies quietly in its heart.

It is acknowledged that handling leaves magnetic vibrations which, mingled with the Seer's, cause much confusion that is not only worthless but detrimental to all concerned.

If a person is equipped to become a consulting Scryer, then that person must be strong enough to firmly but kindly refuse to allow the Crystal Ball to be taken up in unfamiliar hands. When William Shakespeare admonished Laertes in *Hamlet* (Act 1, Scene III), he spoke indirectly to all Scryers:

This above all: to thine own self be true,
And it must follow, as the night the day,
Thou canst not then be false to any man.

When the Crystal Ball is not in use it should be placed on its pedestal in the center of the table. A black silk handkerchief is the perfect cover for it. The cover not only protects the globe from dust, but its more subtle purpose is to refute random reflections which would disturb the rest periods of the Crystal Ball.

Upon leaving the room, the Scryer should further protect the Crystal Ball by locking the door.

How to Use the Crystal Ball

From the beginning of time, the one persistent question has been, "How does one make direct contact with the Crystal Ball?" Immediately three words present themselves—*belief, concentration* and *patience.* All three are equally important; Seership depends upon them. If an individual has an inborn ability to fix the mind or to concentrate, that person is well on the way to becoming a Scryer.

However, none of the three will be as effective if the Seer is not at ease physically. A posture chair will free the Scryer from being distracted by seeking a more comfortable position.

Nothing is more vital than the breath, which is the source of all energy. It behooves every Seer to learn to control the breath and to make it a habit. All professional Seers, like all professional Clairvoyants, cultivate deep breathing for they are aware their psychic powers are enhanced by their lung capacity. Deep breathing is a great aid to concentration, just as physical ease helps erase irritability, and assures a patient attitude.

The time-factor enters strongly into Gazing. There are three periods during the day that are ideal to consult the Crystal Ball—Sunrise, Mid-day, and Sunset. It is generally accepted that Sunrise is the most propitious, for it symbolizes a new beginning. This does not preclude other hours between dawn and dark.

There are definite times to avoid using the Crystal Ball. Those are the dark hours from nine o'clock in the evening, until dawn. During that period the Scryer is renewing vital powers, either through sleep or meditation.

If a person is inclined to mischievousness or even wickedness, it is necessary to warn that individual of the potential dangers of misusing the Crystal Ball. If the Seer's purpose is to malign, eventually a disastrous and regrettable effect will be the outcome. This is not to infer that a Seer must pose as a "goody-goody"—far from it. A Scryer should be an even-tempered, intelligent, joyous, unselfish being. As was previously indicated, consistent use of the Crystal Ball has improved the health and augmented the vital powers.

Interpretation of Phenomena Seen in the Crystal Ball

Clouds

Generally, the first thing of which a novice becomes conscious is a clouding of the Crystal Ball. This clouding may appear in various forms: 1. as a milky obscurity; 2. as a smoky impenetrable mist; 3. as minuscule white clouds drifting through the Crystal Ball. *White clouds are an affirmative indication of coming favors.*

If a brilliance breaks through the clouds, it is indicative of the Sun, *which will light the way to better financial circumstances and to improved physical health.*

However, if a soft light lacking brilliance appears through the clouds, it is indicative of the Moon, *which foretells a period of inaction that may be likened to recuperating the vital forces.*

When the cloud is Black, that is the time to be concerned, for a *Black Cloud is unfavorable, even ill-omened.* The seriousness of the prediction is measured by the degree of blackness. Does the blackness appear in a small portion of the Crystal Ball, or does it fill the entire globe?

Occasionally, the clouds take on a show of color. If Green, Blue, or Violet suffuse the Crystal Ball, this is an excellent indication. *When Green clouds appear,* the individual will be called upon to assist as a neighborhood mediator in an educational, political or religious capacity. *If a Blue cloud appears,* an occasion will arise which requires shrewd discernment, that brings both honor and praise to the individual. *When a Violet cloud floats through the Crystal Ball,* a latent talent may be recognized, or a worthy philosophical expression will be presented and well received.

When clouds of *Red, Orange* or *Yellow* appear the portents are ominous. *Red clouds foretell dangerous situations*—accidents, serious illness and grief. *Orange clouds predict* loss of material goods as well as loss of friendships. *Yellow clouds bring* deception and ultimate betrayal by supposed friends.

Directions

Clouds that move upward in the Crystal Ball are positive signs. The questions may regard anything that is uppermost in the interrogator's mind; e.g., *business, health, housing, matrimony, social activities or any of a myriad subjects.*

Clouds that move downward in the Crystal Ball are negative. *Every question earns a ''no''.* However, it must be realized that it is the question itself that causes the cloud to appear and descend.

Clouds that move to the right of the Seer announce the presence of *Spiritual Beings. They are benign, and insure their willingness to assist both the Seer and the individual seeking assistance.*

Clouds that move to the left of the Seer indicate a refusal to continue the ''sitting'' at that time. DO NOT BE DISCOURAGED! Arrange another séance with the Scryer in the near future.

Often it is necessary to look to far-distant places for a complete answer. Under such circumstances look into the Crystal Ball from a lengthwise angle. (*Note:* It may require practice on the part of the Seer to learn to gaze lengthwise. It is well to practice before receiving a client.) Distance is not a determent to the Crystal Ball, for in its unfathomable depth reposes the whole of Creation.

The images which appear on the right hand of the Seer are symbolic; e.g., a ring may indicate an engagement; a briefcase may portend a business appointment; a flower may be interpreted in several ways according to the interests of a client, who may be interested in gardens, or may be considering marriage, or is celebrating a birthday. Symbols and their interpretations are endless.

The images which appear to the left of the Scryer are the actual pictures of objects significant in the interrogator's life.

Also, both the symbolic pictures and the factual pictures may assume the colors which appeared in the clouds, and have a similar effect. For instance, if a reddish car appears, an accident may be imminent. However, if a green car should appear, its errand in all probability is for a good cause; e.g., corresponding to the owner's position in life.

The Search for the Secret of Crystal Gazing

Some form of Crystal Gazing has been recognized since the Ancients used ice for divination. As time passed and ice gave way to quartz, there was even more interest in the Crystal Ball. In the Middle Ages elaborate rituals were invoked before the Seer took up the Crystal Ball, prayerfully read the symbols which appeared, and believed they had heavenly origin.

Naturally there is the skeptic who dismisses the whole thing with a shrug, and claims it is due to the working of an immature mind that is too easily hoaxed. Fortunately, however, there is that rare individual with a thoroughly scientific attitude who endeavors to search for the truth, and refuses to give credence to his own doubts. Such individuals in high places are now looking at the Crystal Ball with renewed interest.

Lewis Spence, one of the world's foremost scholars of occult science has this to say in his *An Encyclopedia of Occultism,* "The object of crystal gazing . . . . is the induction of an hypnotic state giving rise to visionary hallucinations, the reflection of light in the crystal forming *points de repére* for such hallucinations." Later, he says, "There are many well-attested cases wherein the crystal has been successfully used for the purpose of tracing criminals, or recovering lost or stolen property."

While the present-day Seer gives the Crystal Ball all the attention the long-ago Scryer did, ritual has little place in the sittings. For instance, in the early Seventies, the author was privileged to accompany a Seer to an executive building in Westchester County, New York. Within a short time, three of the Company's Presidents had died, apparently of the same illness, which the attending physicians had found puzzling. The three men had occupied the same suite. The man selected to assume the Presidency had qualms about accepting the position.

When the president-to-be recalled an acquaintance who was a respected Seer, he hastily invited him to visit the building. Upon arrival it was noticeable that the grass outside the part of the building in question was brown and dying, and a young tree nearby was drooping and dropping leaves. With no preamble, the Seer took from a pocket a small leather case, from which he lifted a magnificent, unblemished Crystal Ball the size of a child's marble. It was suspended from a ring of minuscule gold lilies. Almost immediately that beautiful clear crystal globe became a dull gray, as if a dark cloud passed through it. What appeared to be a small yellow stone became visible off left center. Quickly the Seer demanded to be taken to the room which overlooked the yard where we stood. Eight paces from the window the yellow object deepened in color, and the gray cloud darkened. The Seer said, "There is an underground stream here from which noxious vapors are rising. It should be a simple matter to correct this." Gently and carefully he returned the Crystal Ball to its velvet lined box.

This proved true. After an excavation revealed the stream, and it was successfully diverted, the grass grew outside the window, the tree became healthy, and the newly-appointed President remained in excellent health. *However, the point is, there was no ritual to invoke the Crystal Ball. Obviously the Seer had perfect rapport with his Crystal, and he knew it.*

Another extraordinary demonstration of Crystal Gazing, which is a proven fact, was the locating of the present Dalai Lama—the Fourteenth. Each Dalai Lama is the reincarnation of his predecessor. Recently the Thirteenth Dalai Lama had died and the immediate search for his reincarnation began. Undeniable evidence led to the belief that the child would be found in the East. This time the crystal ball was *the picturesque Lake Lhamoi Latso at Chokhorgyal.* (*Note:* According to John Melville, water has been used effectively in lieu of quartz.) The Tibetans believed that visions of the future may be seen in this beautiful lake, so the Regent journeyed ninety miles southeast to Chokhorgyal. He spent several days at Lake Lhamoi Latso in meditative prayer. Then the Regent saw the vision—a great monastery with green and gold roofs, and close by a dwelling with turquoise tiles. To the last detail the vision was correct, and the young boy who was destined to be the Dalai Lama was found living with his parents and siblings in the house with the turquoise tiles.

*

In this scientific age many attempts have been made to explain the appearance of clouds and pictures in the Crystal Ball. The question most often voiced is, "Is it possible for a Crystal Ball to pass through physical changes, especially if it has been used for an extended period?" Andrew Lang, who wrote learnedly on crystal gazing, remarked especially on the "milky obscurity" which seemed to pervade the Crystal Ball. When he wrote about crystal gazing, W.R. Newbold also commented on the "milky masses." This led some to believe that self-hypnosis on the part of the Scryer produced the manifestations, which were illusions. Immediately, this conclusion was discarded by dedicated Seers.

However, our endeavor to solve an age-old problem begins with a demanding "WHY?" The Seers have begun to look fearlessly and eagerly into the cause of the manifestations.

It is conceded that visible objects *are* moved by psychokinetic energy. There are numerous cases on record to verify this. Since it is an undeniable fact that psychokinetic energy moves visible objects, then it is feasible that invisible molecules may be manipulated by that same energy; e.g., regrouping atomistic objects to form patterns or pictures or to cloud the Crystal Ball according to the Seer's concentrative power.

Still another question presents itself, "Why are the images in the Crystal Ball so ephemeral?" There is the possibility that as soon as the Seer has received his answer, it becomes part of his store of knowledge and needs no further outward preservaion. It may be likened to a problemic equation on a blackboard which has served its purpose. The blackboard is then cleared for the next example. So long as the Seer concentrates, the molecules regroup themselves until the sitting is closed.

Crystallography, the science which deals with the system of configuration among crystals, their structure and forms of aggregation, verifies the resilence and cohesion in crystals. This geological evidence proves further that the images in the Crystal Ball are not illusions.

Once it has been acknowledged that psychokinetic energy affects matter, it follows that use of the mind's psychic force combined with the sensitive Crystal Ball is incalculable.

The present-day Scryer is in an enviable position. What man has done with the Crystal Ball while being unaware of the psychokinetic energy working through it, and while being unaware, also, of the efficiency of his marvelous brain power to direct it, is not to be compared with the promise of the future use of the Crystal Ball.

Dr. James Hyslop foresaw this Renaissance of Crystal Gazing when he said in his *Enigmas of Psychical Research* (1906): "The incidents in crystal vision apparently showing supernormal acquisition of knowledge so far transcend all that we ordinarily know of acute sensibility that we can only use this last fact (that the limits of knowledge are not confined by normal sensation and perception) as evidence of the possibility of much more besides, and prosecute our inquiries until we find a pathway into the deeper mysteries of the mind."

Early Advocates of the Crystal Ball

Bacon, Roger (1214-1272) most gifted man of the 13th century. He made a "marvelous glass" which pictured events happening at a far-distanced place.

Cagliostro (real name Guiseppe Balsamo) Italian (1743-1795).

Dee, Dr. John (1527-1593?) He experimented in crystallomancy.

Faustus, Dr. (16th century) He gave directions for the preparations of a crystal, whether glass or quartz.

John of Salisbury (1120?-1180) He practiced divination by means of the crystal.

Jami (1414-1492) Poet and Mystic. In his poem, *Salaman & Absal,* he wrote about the magic mirror.

Na-a-che (19th century) He was an Apache Medicine Man who used a crystal.

Paracelsus (1493-1541) He wrote, *How to Conjure the Crystal So That All Things May Be Seen In It.*

Scott, Sir Walter (1771-1852) Poet and novelist. In his time the crystal globe was known among the Scottish Highlanders as "Stones of Power."

Skelhorn, Sarah (16th century) A noted scryer, who had regular employment, for it was customary to have a household seer if it could be afforded.

Bibliography

Aubrey, John. MISCELLANIES. London, 1890.

Besterman, Theodore. CRYSTAL GAZING. William Ryder & Sons, London, 1924.

Glanvil, Joseph. SADDUCISMUS TRIUMPHATUS. London, 1726.

Hyslop, James H. ENIGMAS OF PSYCHICAL RESEARCH. Boston, 1906.

Kunz, George Frederick. THE CURIOUS LORE OF PRECIOUS STONES. J.B. Lippincott, Philadelphia, 1913.

Lang, Andrew. THE MAKING OF RELIGION. London, 1908.

Melville, John. CRYSTAL GAZING & CLAIRVOYANCE. Samuel Weiser, York Beach, Maine, 1974.

Morrill, Sibley S. THE MYSTERY OF CRYSTAL GAZING—HOW AN ANCIENT MAYAN SKULL MAY BE THE KEY. Cadleon Pub. Co., San Francisco, California 94101.

Sepharial, THE CRYSTAL AND THE SEER. London, 1900(?).

Spence, Lewis. AN ENCYCLOPEDIA OF OCCULTISM. University Books, New York, 1960.

Thomas, N.W. CRYSTAL GAZING. London, 1908.